Th

Richard Bell

Pandora's island, Crazy Helen and a castle that never was; discover a thousand years of history in a hundred acres of parkland in the City of Wakefield's Thornes, Clarence and Holmfield Parks.

This one hour stroll starts and finishes at Stork Lodge gates. You'll walk 1½ miles, climbing (then descending) 130 feet. Points of interest are numbered in the text and on the trail map on the back cover.

ISBN 978-1-902467-03-0
First published 1999, revised edition 2008
Willow Island Editions, 41 Water Lane,
Middlestown, Wakefield, WF4 4PX
www.willowisland.co.uk

For Diana & Malcolm

The View from Lowe Hill

'JANE AND ELIZABETH and I walked to Lowe Hill,' wrote **Clara Clarkson** in her diary for Friday 26th July 1833, 'It was a lovely clear evening and the view was beautiful but there were such queer looking men there that we were afraid and walked quickly along the bridge to Dirtcar.'

Her cousin, **Henry Clarkson**, *(1801-1896)* recalled that 'Lowe Hill was a contested place between Wakefield and Thornes. On public holidays such as Easter Monday and Whitsuntide it was a regular battle-field, the contest being sharply waged between Thornes and Wakefield lads. Stones were freely used by

the combatants and the victorious party would chase the fleeing forces into Thornes or the confines of Wakefield, as the case might be. I have joined these mimic battles with my school fellows, the Holdsworths and the Burrells and given and received many an awkward blow.'

Views drawn from the hill in the 1840s and 1860s show a rapidly-changing scene; long chimneys and new railways increasingly dominate the landscape, while Victorian couples stroll through cow pastures.

In the 1850s **Jose Luis Fernandes** suggested a public park on Lowe Hill. In 1887 Wakefield's **Paxton Society** promoted the scheme to celebrate Queen Victoria's Golden Jubilee.

Clarence Park was opened on 6th July 1893, **Holmfield** on Peace Day, 19th July 1919, while **Thornes Park** opened as a public park on August 2nd 1924, during the General Strike.

The first park superintendent, **Mr W H Garside**, transformed pasture into city park by planting 14,098 trees valued at £312.10s.8d. **Sycamore, Horse Chestnut** and **Turkey Oak** were chosen for their ability to withstand smoke and cold. A double row of 108 chestnuts lined the new Carriage Drive in Clarence Park and 36 oaks were planted on the Grand Promenade near the park's first bandstand on top of Lowe Hill.

Thorn, Holm & Lawe

The name **Thornes** probably goes back to Viking times. As you would expect, it means *'thorn'* or *'thorn tree'*. **Thorn** is also a letter in the runic alphabet; Þ, representing a soft 'th' sound.

Holm, as in Holmfield, is Viking for an *'island'* - that is, land raised above flood level - or a *'water meadow'*.

A **Lawe**, Lowe or Low is a *'low hill'* or *'burial cairn'* in both Viking (*lagr*) and Anglo-Saxon (*lah* or *lech*).

Gill Sike, the stream that supplies the park's fish pond, is Viking for *'a narrow stream in a ditch'*.

Strethagh, a long narrow strip of land north of Lowe Hill (1337), is Anglo-Saxon for *'the enclosure (haga) of the old straight (Roman) road'*.

Erlesing (1333), between Thornes and Wakefield, now the Ings Road area, was the Earl de Warenne's *'water meadow'*.

1. Stork Lodge

Thornes Park gate lodge, built in 1842, is now the Stork Lodge Café.

Two metal storks which stood on the gate posts (but which now flank the entrance to the Rose Garden) are from the crest of the Gaskell family, who lived in Thornes House. Local tradition had it that when the storks heard the town hall clock strike midnight, they flew down and paddled in the lake.

They were re-cast from the originals in 1999.

Each stork holds a scallop shell, a symbol of pilgrimage and of St James the Great, who, according to legend, made a miraculous sea journey from the Holy Land to the Spanish coast near his shrine at Santiago de Compostela. Thornes Church is dedicated to this Apostle.

Mr Pugh, an estate worker, lived in the lodge prior to 1919. In Victorian times the lodge had, alongside it, a small square garden neatly divided up by diagonal paths.

At this time Thornes Road was unsurfaced, with a flagstone footpath running by the park wall and a ditch on the opposite side of the road.

2. The Fish Pond

Canada Geese, **Mallard** and **Moorhen** are amongst the regulars on the park lake. A boathouse stood at the lower end of the lake until about 1960. On a map of 1890 the lake is marked as a fish pond while a second, smaller, lake extends upstream almost as far as the gardener's house. This was filled in around 1970. There had been a waterfall between the two.

A statue of **Pandora** stood on the larger island in a little temple. Pandora is the 'Eve' of Greek mythology; Zeus created her to have beauty, grace, intelligence . . . and the power to deceive. Her draped figure held Pandora's box, from which all the evils of the world flew forth, until only Hope remained inside.

No-one knew how old she was, where she came from

or even, for certain, who she was. The Temple, which was marked on a map of 1851, fell into rather dilapidated condition and was eventually destroyed in a gale prior to 1970.

The **Gill Sike** stream which feeds the lake, rises in **Snapethorpe** (Viking; *Sneypis hamlet*) and flows to the Calder. It is now almost entirely hidden from view.

3. The Gardener's House

John Wilson, head gardener to the Gaskells of Thornes House, lived here with his family in 1913. Behind the house they had a pig sty, a goathouse, a horse, Old Tim, in his stable and a few hens wandering about. Lady Milnes Gaskell advocated keeping rabbits for food production.

The **Walled Garden** was then the kitchen garden. Peaches, nectarines, pineapples and grapes were grown in a range of greenhouses. Figs, pears and Morello cherries grew out of doors.

Nearer to Thornes House there were glasshouses for carnations, camellias and orchids. Oranges, palms, ferns and banana plants were grown in the conservatory. In June 1801, nineteen boxes of fruit, including 60 lb. of grapes were dispatched to London for a 'Hot Supper', given by Mrs Milnes, the lady of the house at the time, to celebrate the birthday of King George.

German prisoners of war, who were probably billeted at Lofthouse, worked on the estate during the 1914-18 war.

The fountain in the Walled Garden was restored in 1998.

'Gaskell's Homers' or 'Gaskell's Roamers' was what the locals called the **Rooks** that nested in a large rookery in Thornes Park. Organised shoots helped keep their numbers in check.

A small **dairy** stood between Thornes House and Horbury Road. It had stained glass windows and a Biblical quote about milk and honey carved above the entrance.

*Cockatiels and budgerigars are kept in the park **aviary**. The old spreading tree is a **Laburnum**.*

4. Geordie's Grave

A Victorian pet cemetery lies to the left of the path that goes up behind the aviary. The headstones commemorate **Geordie**, **Jack** *(1896-1910)* and **Sin** *(d. 1901)*, while the largest is inscribed simply to **'My Mouse'**. Here's a suggested translation of the Latin inscription on Geordie's headstone:

GEORDIE
(1868-1882),

He rests among beloved seats of love,
To whom the Fates granted to enjoy nearly thrice times five years.
Having been snatched away in venerable old age he leaves this dear place to us,
Nor did his heart lack faith, ever mindful dog.

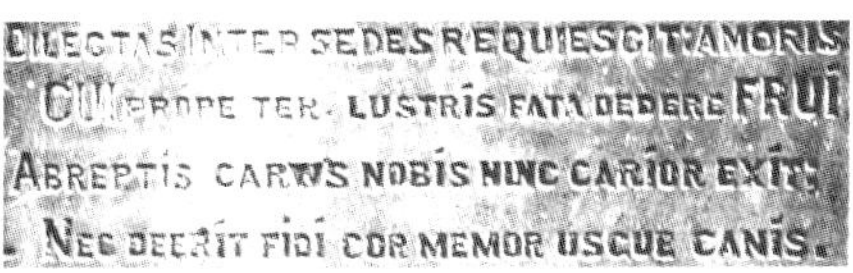

5. Thornes House

after George Richardson, *Vitruvius Britanicus*

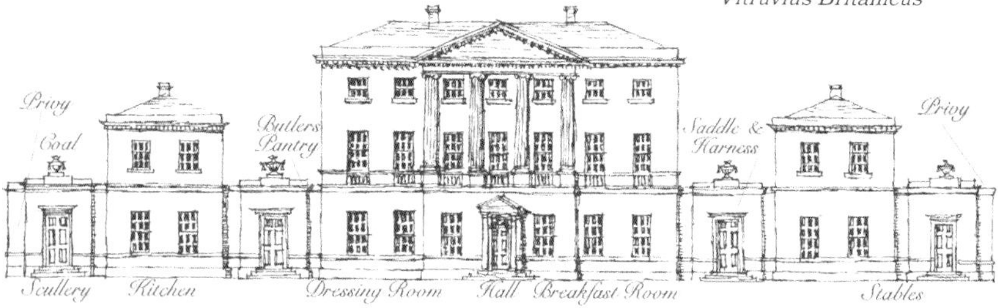

Thornes House was built in 1779-81 to a design by Horbury born architect **John Carr** for cloth merchant **James Milnes** *(1755-1805)* of Westgate, Wakefield. Carr started his career as a quarryman and mason, but for this house, with its 200 ft facade, he used red brick, perhaps made at the Milnes family's brickworks on nearby Westgate Common.

The timber may have been imported from Russia, where the Milnes family had cornered the market in woollen cloth with the sanction of Empress **Catherine the Great** herself.

John Carr (1723-1807)

The butler's pantry was tucked behind the back stairs, near Mr Milnes' dressing room. But the butler, **Robert Crowder**, went on to greater things; in 1802 he left to take the Strafford Arms in Wakefield's Bull Ring where he was so success-

Parts of the retaining wall of the terrace (left) remain.

ful that he was able to retire and build himself a comfortable house; Castle Lodge at Sandal, where he died in 1823.

The last occupant of Thornes House was **Charles George Milnes Gaskell** *(1842-1919)*, M.P. for Morley *(1885-92)*, chairman of the West Riding County Council and a Privy Councillor. At the suggestion of his wife, **Lady Catherine**, the house was used as a military hospital during the First World War. In 1919 Wakefield Corporation bought house and land for £18,500, intending to build 750 council houses in the park.

The site was the home of **Thornes House School** from 1921 until 1993 and was then occupied by **Wakefield College**.

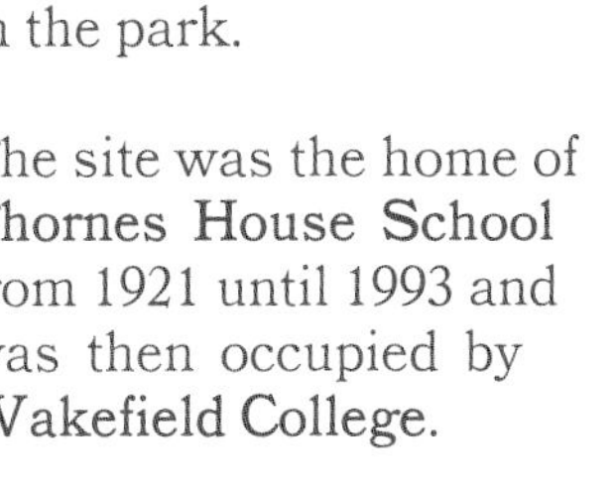

Charles George Milnes Gaskell

A Midsummer Mystery

MYSTERY surrounds the blaze that destroyed Thornes House one Saturday night in July 1951. It had been a warm evening so members of the **Wakefield Amateur Theatre Guild** had been able to perform their production of *A Midsummer Night's Dream* out of doors in the park. The actors, using the house as a dressing room, were the last people known to have legitimately used the building.

One of the main characters in the *Dream* is **Puck**, or Robin Goodfellow, a Goblin; a kind of familiar demon, dwelling, according to popular legend, in private houses, chinks of trees and various other places.

Just across the River Calder lies the **Pugneys** which is Anglo Saxon for *Puck's* (püca's) *water meadows*. In such areas marsh gas can give rise to will o' the wisp lights while vegetation poor in calcium can lead to brittle bones in cattle. Pigmy flints, like those found at the Pugneys and on Lowe Hill, were once called 'elf arrows', supposedly shot by the little people at cattle or men out of malice or revenge. A cow, or person, afflicted by a mysterious ailment had been 'elf-shot'.

'I am feared in field and town,' says Puck in the play; *'Sometime a horse I'll be, sometime . . . a headless bear, sometime a fire; And neigh, . . and roar, and burn'.* At the end of the play, after a supernatural blessing on a house, the mischievous Puck has the last word; *'Robin shall restore amends.'*

A few hours later the blaze started! Firemen pumped water from the Park Lake to douse the flames. Detectives found signs of a break-in and jemmy marks on the school safe.

Track Events

The **Wakefield Society of Model and Experimental Engineers** carried their first passenger in Thornes Park in June 1958. The present ground level track is 7¼ inch gauge and about half a mile long.

Before the days of steam, **Smithson's Rail Road** *(c.1798-1869)*, ran past this corner of the park. Horses hauled the laden wagons from collieries at Low Laithes to Thornes Wharf. Local historian S. Baines recalled that village boys occasionally hopped on the back of the laden trucks.

The sports centre and track were constructed in the 1990s. There are now plans to relocate **Trinity Wildcats** rugby league club to the park. In the final of the Yorkshire Challenge Cup on April 1st 1882 **Thornes Rugby Team** unexpectedly defeated Wakefield Trinity in the Final of 'T'owd Tin Pot' **Yorkshire Challenge Cup.** H. Dawson made the mark and H. Wigglesworth scored the only goal. Trinity scored one try.

The Stable Block

The **stable block**, now demolished, stood by the driveway at the top of the slope. It contained loose boxes, harness rooms and grooms' quarters and had a house attached to it. The clock on the tower was black with gold numerals. There were saw pits and drying posts nearby and an ice house, built partly underground.

In due course the Gaskells obtained a car, and appointed a Mr East as their chauffeur.

Crab apple trees lined the driveway leading up from Stork Lodge. The fruit was used for making crab apple jelly. In 1923 there were still pheasants, hares and rabbits in all three parks.

The **Park Lodge** at the Lawfield Lane entrance to Clarence Park was built in 1897 at the expense of Charles George Milnes Gaskell, chairman of the park trustees. The gate lodge at the Horbury Road entrance to Thornes Park, now demolished, was a less convenient home; the living room and bedroom were on opposite sides of the drive.

6. Ridge & Furrow

On the slopes and plateau of **Lowe Hill** there are long strips that look, to me, like **ridge and furrow** cultivation*, traces of the medieval open fields of Thornes. Near the top you can see two sets of strips, one set running up the slope from Lawefield Lane, the other running almost at right angles along the crest of the ridge. A rough area between may be the headland where the plough teams turned. The strips are about 7½ yards wide. A map of 1753 by John Dickinson shows the 'Law Field' with gentle reverse S-bends on the strips, caused by the team of oxen starting to turn.

In 1297 small numbers of pigs, horses, cattle and sheep were kept in the district. More oats were grown than wheat (three times the quantity). Farmers were obliged to take their grain for milling at the Earl's water-mill at Wakefield Bridge End. The farmers of the oxgang lands at Thornes had the additional responsibility of repairing the mill dam.

In 1347 the rents paid to the last Earl de Warenne for Thornes amounted to £8. Neighbouring Alverthorpe paid only £6.8s., but also supplied the Earl with hens and eggs.

**the alternative suggestion of 18th century land drainage seems unlikely on the summit plateau.*

7. Lowe Hill

A print of 1722 shows two horsemen and a pack of hounds chasing a hare across the slopes of Lowe Hill. When Thornes House was built in 1779-81 it was still possible for a sportsman to 'go out on the common for an hour or two before breakfast, and return with a hare and two or three brace of birds.'* There were Snipe on the marshy areas.

The open land of **Thornes Moor**, **Westgate Common** and **Whinney Moor** stretched from Westgate Bridge to Lupset. Westgate Common was enclosed in 1793-4.

Supporting the campaign against the enclosure of Heath Common in 1844 **Charles Waterton** asked 'once merry Wakefield say, what is to become of thy Fifteen Thousand People, who will have not a yard of public land remaining, whereon to recover that health of frame, and vigor of the mind, so apt to be enfeebled when debarred from the advantage of rural air and pastime ?'

Charles George Milnes Gaskell sold Lowe Hill for use as a park on October 13th 1899.

In his *History of Wakefield* Walker states that a beacon fire was lit on the summit of Lowe Hill in 1588 to warn of the Spanish Armada.

 *Clarkson, *Memories of Merry Wakefield*

The Castle on Lowe Hill

1722

'A QUARTER of a mile without Wakefield,' says **Leland**, writing in 1538; 'appeareth a hill of earth cast up, where some say that one of the Earls Warren began to build, and as fast as he builded violence of wind defaced the work. This is like a fable. Some say that it was nothing but a windmill hill. This place is now called Lo-Hill.'

'Those that say it is nothing but a wind-mill are surely mistaken' wrote the **Rev. Benjamin Forster** in 1766. The name '*Lowe*' suggests there may once have been an ancient burial cairn here.

The castle was probably built by **William, 3rd Earl de Warenne**, Lord of the Manor of Wakefield. He died in 1148 while fighting on a crusade in Turkey. His head was brought back to England for burial in Lewes Priory.

In 1324 Edward II gave the care of the castles (plural) of Wakefield *and* Sandal to Richard de Moseley. In 1330 a Great Gale damaged the mills and bridges of the town and after this no more is heard of the Wakefield castle. It was probably timber built and never permanently occupied.

Brian Hope-Taylor found medieval pottery and a spur when he excavated the earthworks on the hilltop in 1953. He suggested that a castle was probably built here towards the end of the civil war between King Stephen and the 'Empress' Matilda *(1139-54)*.

Saints & Scallops

'Crazy Helen's Walk', an ancient pathway across Lowe Hill, was closed in 1869. A centuries old tree known as **Crazy Helen** or Crazy Nell stood in Holmfield Park. It was partly uprooted in 85 mph winds in a gale on October 29th 1927 but an old hollow tree, in which a wild woman was said to have lived, could still be seen here in the 1950s.

Why should the name Helen be associated with an ancient path across a hill? **Helen** was the Celtic goddess of the holy road and there is a Sarn Helen, '*Helen's Causeway*' in Wales but another possibility is **St Helen**, to whom Sandal Church is dedicated; according to tradition, Empress Helena *(c.248-c.328)*, mother of Constantine the Great, discovered the True Cross in Jerusalem and founded the basilica on the Mount of Olives in 326. In the Middle Ages, she was believed to be a native of Britain.

The Gaskell family's **scallop** shell crest links Thornes with the Apostle St James the Great. **St Joseph of Arimathea** was a contemporary of St James, and, like him, is traditionally credited with a sea journey from the Holy Land. Bringing the Holy Grail with him, he is said to have founded an Abbey at a site rather similar to Lowe Hill; at Glastonbury, where an isolated hill with a well at its foot, overlooks marshy meadows. Thorn trees have a special significance at Glastonbury, as they evidently had at Thornes.

Seal of John, 8th and last Earl de Warenne, Lord of the Manor of Wakefield

The Earl's Deer

In January 1285 Richard de Hey was charged with taking the Earl's deer at Thornes with traps made of great cords. Richard said that he had taken, and intended to take whenever he could, all deer found in his close, because that was his common chase.

The **drinking fountain** was erected 1893 in memory of **Major Barker** of Holmfield House, by the work-force of his worsted mill at Thornes Wharf.

The **horse trough** once stood on Westgate. It was erected in 1888 by members of the RSPCA as a tribute to the work of **Ann Clarkson** of Westgate Bridge.

'Cousin Ann *(then aged 76)* called,' writes Clara Clarkson in her diary for March 14th, 1876. 'She told me that as she passed the top of Salt-pie Alley *(which still exists, between the Smith's Arms and Westgate Retail Park)* she saw an Irishman beating his wife and she interfered and he struck her a nasty blow on the arm. All her life Ann has interfered when she saw anyone being cruel to animals and people have always deferred to her but this man frightened her. I really believe it was the first time in her life that she was afraid; perhaps the man was in drink.'

Prince 'Jack'?!

On 30th April 1891 **Prince Albert Victor, Duke of Clarence & Avondale**, *(1864-1892)* son of Edward, the Prince of Wales, planted a white horse chestnut tree at the foot of Lowe Hill. **Clarence Park** was officially opened two years later on July 6th 1893 by Charles George Milnes Gaskell of Thornes House.

The Prince, known as 'Eddy' to his friends, is the highest ranking suspect in Jack the Ripper conspiracy theories. Films, television shows, comic books and novels have implicated him in the murders. However, as in all the best conspiracies, the Prince has the perfect alibi; he was having lunch with Queen Victoria, his grandmother, at Abergeldie, Scotland, on 30th September 1888, the day that two of the victims were murdered in the East End of London.

This theory is largely based on a story, featured in a 1973 BBC television production, that the painter Walter Sickert *(1860-1944)* is said to have told his son, Joseph. Joseph later retracted the story. In her 2002 book Patricia Cornwell asserts that Walter Sickert himself was the killer.

The Prince's tree never thrived and the Prince himself died in the 'flu epidemic of 1891-2.

The Clarence Park Cannon

A statue of **Queen Victoria** was erected in 1904 and unveiled in the Bull Ring in Wakefield, in 1905. She was removed to Clarence Park on July 10th 1950 and stood here until November 1984, when she was returned, after cleaning, to the Bull Ring.

A **brass cannon** seized from the Russians at the fall of Sebastopol, September 8th 1855, once stood on the top of Lowe Hill, near the original bandstand. It had been tested in the presence of Emperor Nicholas I *(1796-1855)* and bore the Imperial arms of Russia.

It was fired on Wakefield Ings on the afternoon of Monday 6th September 1858 as the royal train took Queen Victoria through Wakefield on her way to Leeds, where she was to open the Town Hall. The sound reverberated around the town. The queen was seen to stand up in the carriage to see what the commotion was.

It originally stood outside the Court House in Wakefield. When pranksters charged it up and fired it, albeit blank, windows were smashed and nearby buildings shaken.

The cannon was spiked and removed to Lowe Hill, to stand near the original bandstand. It was, apparently, taken for scrap during World War II.

8. Thornes Church

THE CHURCH of St James *(built 1829-30)* was the last of the 'Million' churches built in Wakefield, after Stanley *(1822-4)* and Alverthorpe *(1823-5)*. The £1,000,000 fund, assigned by Parliament for the provision of new churches in populous areas, was part of a war indemnity paid by Austria after the Battle of Waterloo. One thousand pounds was paid from the fund, but the greater part of the £2,035 cost was met by Benjamin Gaskell *(1781-1856)* of Thornes House.

In 1895 the church's pulpit was replaced by one from the Queen Elizabeth Grammar School. The bottom section of the old pulpit, turned upside down, was used as a summerhouse for many years by 'Old Mr Tunnicliffe', corn miller and amateur weather prophet, who lived in a stone cottage just north of the church.

As a welcome ritual, the choir boys threw new recruits from the top of the churchyard wall into the middle of a particularly prickly holly bush.

While digging a grave in the sandy soil of the churchyard Mr Rowe, the verger, (who was cowman to the Gaskells), was trapped when the sides of the grave caved in on him. Luckily, after some time, his cries for help were answered. In 1850 the fee for digging a grave at Thornes was three shillings (15 pence).

The **Church Parochial Hall** next door (now Howarth Funeral Service's Chapel of Rest) was built in 1911 at a cost of £1,300, which included the site. The foundation stone was laid by Lady Catherine Milnes Gaskell of Thornes House.

There is a suggestion that Thornes **Vicarage** was built on a grand scale in 1840 at the expense of the

Thornes Vicarage

Gaskells of Thornes House, who hoped to encourage one of their friends to take the Parish. A bazaar at Wakefield's Music Saloon on 12th September 1838 raised £823 towards the project.

Rose Cottage (built prior to 1823) stood next to the iron gates of Clarence Park. The gates were demolished when the Denby Dale Road was widened, the cottage long before that.

9. Bandstand

BAND CONCERTS at the original bandstand on Lowe Hill in 1893 attracted as many as 2,000 people but, because of limited space on the summit terrace, there was a danger of people being jostled down the slope.

The new bandstand opened in 1926 with a concert by Wakefield Old Band. The *Wakefield Express* described the new site at the foot of the hill as 'the finest natural stadium in the country for band music'. Designed by Mr L Ives, the City Surveyor, it cost £1,514 to build. It is faced in part with Accrington brick and stone dressings plus mock-Tudor beams. The shell stage acts as a loudspeaker. Increased traffic on the Denby Dale Road now makes the site less suitable and summer seasons of concerts have been held in the Rose Garden.

The Wakefield Mystery Plays were performed in the Park to mark the Festival of Britain, 1951.

Shelter, Clarence Park

Denby Dale Turnpike Road

An early view of the Denby Dale Road, showing Thornes Church, the Vicarage and Lowe Hill.

A CHAIN of new roads was authorised by Act of Parliament in 1825 to link Wakefield and Barnsley with Manchester. There were toll gates at Ings Road, Thornes Lane and north of the river. Henry Clarkson *(see page 2)* was involved with the survey.

There were problems for the Trustees of the Wakefield and Denby Dale Turnpike Road; the tolls rarely amounted to more than £900 a year, the first clerk William Jackson was dismissed in 1839, owing the Trust over £150, and, in 1836, the flimsy suspension bridge over the Calder collapsed under the weight of a heavily laden barley wagon, drowning three horses.

When the Trust was wound up in 1874 it's said that the Bishop Blaize Inn donated a barrel of beer towards the celebrations in Thornes which continued by torchlight well into the night.

The hedges alongside the road here were once so high that you couldn't see over the top of them. As on Thornes Road, a single row of flags served as a pavement.

Mesolithic quartzite pebble mace head found in 1950 at 95, Thornes Road.

10. Holmfield House

Holmfield House *(Holmfield Arms inn & restaurant)* was built in 1833-34 by solicitor **Thomas Foljambe** *(1775-1851)*, then aged 58. In June the following year Foljambe* became a founder member of the city's Archery Club which met on Heath Common and held an annual competition for a silver arrow trophy. There's a parallel with the Robin Hood silver arrow story: Foljambe had been appointed Deputy Sheriff of the West Riding in 1804. Major Barker, who bought the house for £6,500 in 1863, had it enlarged. An avenue of chestnut trees was planted by his gardener, Mr Denton.

In 1871, in *Walks about Wakefield*, W S Banks describes the house as 'much altered . . . in point of style it is one of the best modern houses in Wakefield.' But he complains of the 'gloomy high wall' that surrounded it. Its attractions included a billiard room, butler's pantry, schoolroom and stillroom. The grounds

 * *or, perhaps, his son of the same name.*

included a vinery and hothouses.

On January 13th 1907 Mr James Wigglesworth of Holmfield hanged himself in the Stables, which stood to the north west of the house.

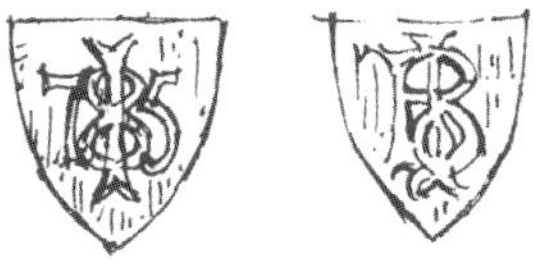

Major Barker's initials and date, 1875

In 1918 Wakefield Corporation agreed to purchase the house for £3,000 with the grounds valued at a further £2,500. From 1923 the upper part was used as the first City Museum.

The **Ginkgo** tree *(a specimen grows near the entrance to Holmfield House)* is a 'living fossil'. Its leaves are almost identical to those found fossilised alongside the dinosaurs. Although it is extinct in the wild it has survived thanks to the old Chinese custom of planting it in temple gardens.

A British **First World War tank**, christened 'Ada' (after the Mayoress) with a bottle of champagne, stood on a concrete plinth in Holmfield Park. Eye-witnesses tell us that, when the tank arrived; 'it did a smart right turn and promptly crashed its way through the Park wall,' which collapsed 'like a pack of cards'. It was removed for scrap in February 1930.

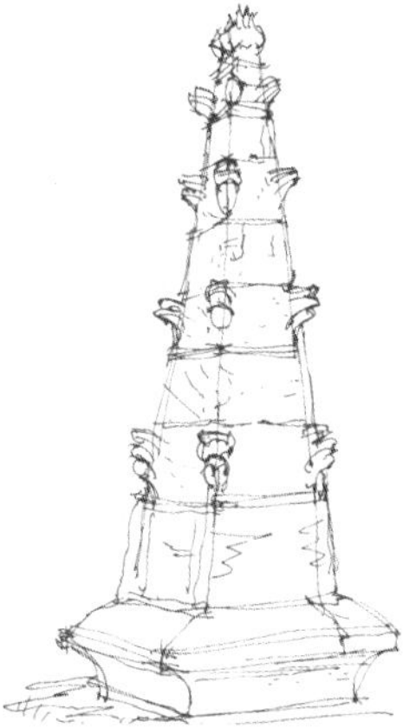

The Rockery

In the 1990s, when the Holmfield House Rockery was demolished to make room for an extension to the hotel (now a Premier Inn), these two items were removed to the garden of Wakefield Art Gallery, Wentworth Terrace:

The **pinnacle** was probably from the Cathedral.

The **Doric pillar** was from Wakefield's Market Cross of 1707, which stood in Cross Square. When the cross was sold in 1866 other pillars went to Alverthorpe Hall and Clarke Hall.

The **archway**, of unknown origin, was re-erected, in truncated form, in the hotel garden at Holmfield.

11. Stocks Hill

The Thornes Road corner of Holmfield Park was once an open area known as **Stocks Hill**. In 1851 Thornes Village School stood here, about where the sports hut now stands. There was a smithy nearby.

In Victorian times, on Cattle Fair days Constable Smith, and a posse of village lads, rounded up any cattle that had strayed from the road and charged one shilling per head for their release from Thornes **Pinfold**, which stood near Stocks Hill.

George Stephenson was the consulting engineer on the Thornes to Horbury stretch of the **Manchester and Leeds Railway** (*c.* 1840). A large house (probably the one on Thornes Lane dated 1839) was built for Mr Foljambe of Holmfield using stone excavated during the making of the tunnel, now Addingford Cutting, at Horbury. The 1926 **railway bridge** contains a girder 96 feet long, weighing 50 tons.

The **rhubarb sculpture** was carved in locally grown oak by Handspring Design of Sheffield to mark the starting point of the Sustrans cycle route to Horbury Junction, which opened in 2005.

12. Thornes Pump

You can see the stone base of the pump from Stocks Hill, diagonally across the Denby Dale Road, beyond the railway bridge. The base was moved a few yards during the 1967-68 development of the dual carriageway. It was erected in 1827, when W Kelshaw was Constable, as was recorded on an iron plate on the pump. It was used until the late 1870s, when a spillage from a cask of paraffin tainted the water.

The **Bishop Blaize Inn**, named after the patron saint of wool-combers, stood nearby. It closed on June 24th 1924, due to the widening of the railway. It had stood there for two centuries and, for half that time, was connected with the Leighton family. Landlord William Leighton died on September 15th 1907, aged 70.

The Bishop Chippy, named after the Bishop Blaize Inn, is now a hot food takeaway.

At Easter in 1315 John Grafford was appointed the ale-taster for Thornes. Ale-tasting seems to have been one of the more popular manorial duties.

Neolithic polished light grey flint axe-head dating from about 2,000 BC. It was found on Avondale Street in 1925 in a spot that was probably once a riverside marsh. It shows no signs of use so might have been an offering at a votive pool.

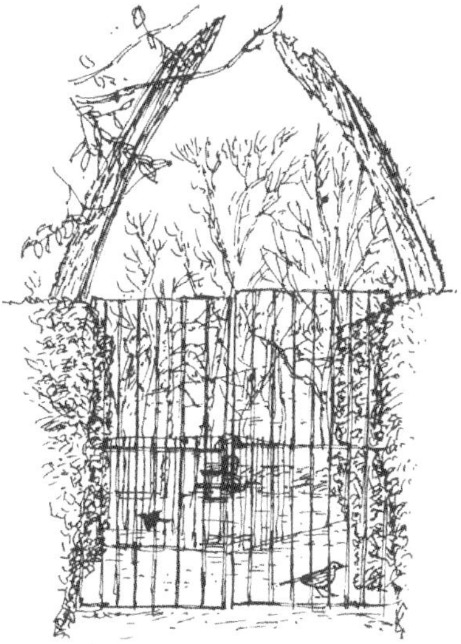

13. Whale Jawbones

Like so much in the park there is a mystery about theses jawbones. Where did they come from? When were they erected? The arch stands over 11 feet high and 7 feet wide, at the entrance to one of the bowling greens. The bones of which it is made are more than a foot broad at the base. They have weathered to a bark-like texture.

They *may* originally have stood at Sandal Castle from 1900 (or earlier) until the late 1930s.

We don't even know what species of whale it was. They may be the bones of a **Fin**, **Sei** or, if they date from the days of sail, a **Greenland Right Whale**, a slow-moving species considered the 'right' whale to catch. The jaws supported baleen plates, a filter system used by the whale to extract krill from the ocean.

At one time there were hundreds of these arches to be seen in Yorkshire, erected as decorative features, the bones being brought back to the whaling ports of Whitby and Hull. Most have now rotted away and this arch is one of only 90 still standing in the U.K.

Holmfield Bowling Green opened on 23rd April 1921. Three thousand games were played in the first two months.

MY THANKS to Ann Barnes, Norah George, John Goodchild, Colin Howes, Linda Ingham, Pam Judkins, Adrian Norris, Nick Redman, Diana and Malcolm Slater, Jeff Stubbs, Andrew Tart, the staff at the Stork Lodge Café and Wakefield MDC Parks Department.

Further Reading

Baines, S., *History of the Village of Thornes*, c. 1920. (manuscript in Wakefield Local Studies Library)
Nora J. George, *Thornes House, the Story of a School*, 1993
John Goodchild, *The Development of Wakefield in maps plans and views, c. 1680 - 1926*, 1981
Hope-Taylor, Brian: *Report on the Excavation at Lowe Hill, Wakefield*, Wakefield Historical Society, 1953
Ronald Pearson & Joe Wilson, *Thornes*, 1976
Kate Taylor, *Wakefield District Heritage, volume 1*, 1976
J. W. Walker *Wakefield its History and People*, 1934

Also by Richard Bell: *Around Old Horbury, Around Old Ossett, Waterton's Park, Sandal Castle, Coxley Valley, Malham Magic, Walks Around Horbury, Walks Around Newmillerdam, Rough Patch, High Peak Drifter, Drawing on Reserves, Yorkshire Rock*

You can still see parts of the balustrade and terrace of Thornes House, now mostly hidden by trees and bushes, (see page 11).